Shipwrecks from the Westward Movement

James P. Delgado

Watts LIBRARY

Franklin Watts
A Division of Grolier Publishing
New York • London • Hong Kong • Sydney
Danbury, Connecticut

To Lynn Vermillion, the first librarian to help me reach for the past

The author would like to thank his wife, Ann Goodhart, whose first professional love was being a children's librarian, who prodded him into writing this book, and who read it through more than once. He would also like to thank Jerry Ostermiller, Leonard McCann, Tom Beasley, John Foster, Stephen R. James, Jack Hunter, Monica Reed Hunter, Harlan Soeten, Richard Everett, Allen Pastron, Tom Layton, and Jacques Marc.

Note to readers: Definitions for words in **bold** can be found in the Glossary at the back of this book.

Photographs ©: BC Archives, Province of B.C.: 3 top, 27 (D-06222), 3 bottom, 24 (F-04359); Bertrand Collection, Desoto National Wildlife Refuge: 53; Culver Pictures: 12, 13; James P. Delgado: 28, 29, 35; Liaison Agency, Inc.: 8, 9, 10, 14, 17 (Hulton Getty); Museum of the Steamboat Arabia, Kansas City, MO: 48, 49, 51 (David Hawley); National Geographic Image Collection: 52 (John Fulton); National Park Service: 54 (J. Livingstone/Submerged Cultural Resources Unit), 4, 18, 19, 21, 22 (Submerged Cultural Resources Unit); North Wind Picture Archives: 16, 32, 40; Royal British Columbia Museum, Victoria, British Columbia: 26 (Photographic Collections, Dd SF1); San Francisco Maritime National Historical Park: 41 (Steve Danford & Tim Campbell), 36, 37; SuperStock: 42, 43 (A.K.G., Berlin); The Bancroft Library, University of California, Berkeley: 30, 31, 39; Thomas N. Layton: 44 (Illustration by S.F. Manning), 6, 45, 46; Underwater Archaeological Society of British Columbia: 47. Cover illustration by Greg Harris.

Visit Franklin Watts on the Internet at: http://publishing.grolier.com

Library of Congress Cataloging-in-Publication Data

Delgado, James P.
    Shipwrecks from the westward movement / James P. Delgado.
        p.   cm.— (Watts Library)
    Includes bibliographical references and index.
    Summary: Describes the excavations of the watercraft of explorers, settlers, and traders who visited the American West from the 1600s to the 1800s and what the findings reveal about life in early America.
    ISBN: 0-531-20380-8 (lib. bdg.)   0-531-16484-5 (pbk.)
    1. West (U.S.)—Discovery and exploration Juvenile literature. 2. West (U.S.)—History—To 1848 Juvenile literature. 3. West (U.S.)—History—1848–1860 Juvenile literature. 4. Shipwrecks—West (U.S.)—History Juvenile literature. 5. Inland navigation—West (U.S.)—History Juvenile literature. 6. Frontier and pioneer life—West (U.S.) Juvenile literature. 7. Excavations (Archaeology)—West (U.S.)— Juvenile literature. [1. West (U.S.)—Discovery and exploration. 2. West (U.S.)—History—To 1848. 3. West (U.S.)—History—1848–1860. 4. Shipwrecks. 5. Frontier and pioneer life—West (U.S.) 6. Excavations (Archaeology) 7. Underwater archaeology. 8. Archaeology.] I. Title. II. Series.
F592.D34 2000
978'.01—dc21   99-25425
                                                                                                    CIP

Contents

In 1978, archaeologists unearthed the whaling ship Niantic in downtown San Francisco.

Learning from the Past

One day in 1978 after I had just started working for the National Park Service in San Francisco, I went to look at a buried ship—downtown. **Archaeologists** were digging it up in the middle of the city's high-rise buildings. As an archaeologist who had worked on land, digging up pre-historic Indian sites and early Spanish settlements, I was interested in what stories this ship would tell. The ship, called the *Niantic*, told us how San Francisco had changed from a small frontier village

This silver and flint tinderbox was among the many artifacts recovered from the Frolic *wreck.*

into a major city. It also told how ships were used in the California Gold Rush—and in the westward movement.

My work on the *Niantic* made me change my focus as an archaeologist from land sites to shipwrecks. Since then, I have worked on shipwrecks all over the world. Many of them have been wrecks in the western United States. And they all tell stories about the westward movement.

The ships that I discuss in this book are very real to me because I have dived on, **excavated**, and studied nearly all of them. I have fought the fast currents of the Columbia River to explore the wreck of the *Isabella*. I have plunged into the deep, cold waters of Burrard Inlet in Vancouver, British Columbia, in Canada, to investigate the steamer *Beaver*'s broken **hull** and machinery. I have dug up and grappled with the thick mud of San Francisco to look at the *Niantic*. I have dived in the Sacramento River to study the *Sterling* and on the California coast to look at the *Frolic*.

Visiting the sites of these ships made their stories come alive for me. That's exciting. And that's why I want to share their stories with you.

—James P. Delgado

Investigating the Past

Archaeologists have been called time detectives. By carefully studying the things left by people of earlier times, archaeologists rediscover lost and forgotten history—and learn how people lived in the past.

Many early explorers, trappers, and traders journeyed west on water.

Chapter One

Shipwrecks on the Frontier

The first Europeans who settled in North America came by sea. Then they left the East Coast and traveled west on foot and by wagon. They also spread across the continent on water. This westward movement left wrecked canoes, riverboats, and ships. Today, archaeologists are rediscovering these wrecks on the bottom of the sea or in lakes and rivers.

Shipwrecks from the westward movement tell us about how pioneers reached the West. They also tell us what goods were brought west to trade or to start a new life on the frontier. The wrecks also tell us about the watercraft—from small canoes to steam-powered riverboats—that helped open the frontier.

The Great Move West

The first people to move into the Far West were fur trappers and traders. Archaeologists diving in the fast-moving rivers that cross the U.S.-Canadian border have discovered places where fur-trade canoes tipped, spilling people and their

Fur traders explored the rivers of North America in birch-bark canoes.

belongings. Other archaeologists working in the waters off Oregon, Washington, and British Columbia have discovered the wrecks of early ships that carried supplies and goods to fur-trading forts on the coast.

Very few people came west to the Pacific Coast until gold was discovered in California in 1848. Thousands then rushed west, both on ships and in wagon trains that crossed the plains. This great move west was called the Gold Rush. Archaeologists have discovered the wrecks of several ships from the Gold Rush, including some ships that were pulled up onto the beach and used as buildings on the frontier.

After the Gold Rush, much of the West remained open for settlement. People still came by wagon, but many people traveled by train. The first railroad to cross the United States completely was finished in 1869. The first railroad to cross Canada was completed in 1887. Many other people came by river, at first in barges and flatboats, and then in big riverboats powered by steam engines.

Changing River Channels

Over time, beaches build up sand, and storms wash it away. Rivers cut new channels when there are floods or when tree branches block the way. Because of these changes, archaeologists sometimes may discover wrecks some way out of the water. Sometimes a shifting beach leaves some wrecks high and dry in a sand dune. And sometimes a new river channel leaves old wrecks buried in mud and sand. In time, this new land may be farmed.

Archaeologists have studied two river steamboats that wrecked on the Missouri River. Over time, they were buried beneath cornfields where the river once flowed. These wrecks of the westward movement are a window to the past.

Many settlers traveled to the western frontier on flatboats loaded with supplies and animals.

An American fur trader with his gun slung over one shoulder

Chapter Two

Fur Traders

The first settlers came west not long after the first European explorers. They were not interested in farming or building cities. They came for fur, which became an important trade item. Either they trapped animals themselves or they traded with the Native Americans for fur. The pelts of the beavers that lived on the banks of the rivers and streams of North America were particularly valuable. The fur trade began in the 1600s and continued into the 1800s. It was one of the longest lasting and most important commercial activities on the frontier.

The Fur Trade

France and Britain controlled the fur trade. Both countries fought many battles in North America to control the trade. They also built forts and other settlements. The fur trade played a crucial role in the development of the United States and Canada.

Fur trade canoes often capsized on dangerous river rapids.

Fur Trade Canoes and Their Goods

The Great Lakes, St. Lawrence River, Ottawa River, and hundreds of streams and lakes form the Quetico-Superior area, located in today's Minnesota and Ontario, Canada. Early fur traders used the waterways there as their highway system. Many fur trade canoes capsized and broke up in the river **rapids**, where the current flows fast, usually over rocks. Archaeologists diving in these rough waters have found traces of many old accidents.

The fragile birch-bark canoes of the fur traders are long gone, smashed and carried away by the strong currents. But archaeologists and local divers have found and recovered many **artifacts** lying on the river bottom. Artifacts—the things people make—can tell us much about the past. Artifacts from the rapids tell us that the early fur traders in the West lived off the land and carried their few belongings in pouches.

In Michigan's Granite River, archaeologists discovered a fur trader's pouch with the remains of an axe, musket balls, lead shot for a gun, a gunflint, and an iron spearhead used to kill muskrats. Divers in other rivers found complete muskets and iron axes—valuable trade items highly prized by the Native Americans. Other unearthed items that were traded for fur include clay pipes, beads, buttons, brass kettles, pigment for painting, and brass thimbles used by Native Americans for sewing decorations. Several iron spearheads show that the fur traders also left goods so that the Native Americans instead of the Europeans could kill muskrats for their fur.

A white hunter taking the hand of a young Native American woman as his wife

Stories of the Past

In time, fur trappers became traders and formed large companies that worked with the Native Americans. Many fur trappers and traders also married local Native American women and settled down to raise families on the frontier. Some of their descendants, known as the Metis, live in Canada today. Their memories of fur-trading ancestors are strong. They add their stories and legends of the past to the work of archaeologists who dig at the sites of the old fur trade forts—and dive into the rapids where canoes spilled their goods centuries ago.

The Hudson's Bay Company built Fort Vancouver on the Columbia River in 1825.

Chapter Three

Wrecked on the Columbia!

The Hudson's Bay Company is North America's oldest company. It was founded in 1670 in England to trade for fur. Over the centuries, the Hudson's Bay Company pushed west, finally reaching the Pacific Ocean in 1821. British, Spanish, French, and Russian explorers had already surveyed the Pacific Coast by sea and land. In 1805, American explorers Meriwether Lewis and William Clark traveled overland to the mouth of the Columbia River.

19

At that time, British and American ships had already been trading for furs on the coast since the 1780s. After Lewis and Clark's **expedition**, New York businessman John Jacob Astor built a fort called Astoria on the Columbia. He sold Astoria to the North West Company, a British fur trading company. The North West Company was a rival of the powerful Hudson's Bay Company. The rivalry ended when the two companies joined in 1821.

The Hudson's Bay Company built a large new fort on the Columbia River in 1825. Fort Vancouver, the first British settlement on the Pacific, was a trading outpost surrounded by a high fence, or stockade. Each year, a ship from Britain sailed to Fort Vancouver with supplies and goods and returned loaded with furs. Although fur traders at the fort grew much of their own food, raised large herds of livestock, and manufactured some goods, they still depended on the supplies from the British ships. The arrival of the annual supply ship was an important event. If it failed to arrive, it could mean disaster for the people at the fort.

The *Isabella* Wreck

In 1829, the British supply ship *William and Ann* wrecked at the mouth of the Columbia River. The crew was killed, and the ship and its valuable cargo were lost.

Hudson's Bay Company officials quickly bought a new ship, the *Isabella*, and loaded it with more supplies and goods. The *Isabella* sailed across the Atlantic, around Cape Horn at the southern tip of South America, and up the Pacific Coast to reach the Columbia River in May 1830. But disaster struck again. The *Isabella*'s captain entered the river the wrong way and hit a huge submerged sandbar. Waves tore off the ship's **rudder**, making it impossible to steer. As water washed over the decks, the crew abandoned the *Isabella*. The ship, half sunk and on its side, washed onto a small island in the river.

Later, the *Isabella* crew went back aboard to retrieve the ship's cargo. They cut a hole into the ship's side to pump out some of the water and pulled everything they could from the ship as it broke apart in the strong river currents.

An underwater view of the hand-cut hole in the Isabella

An archaeological map of the Isabella *site in the Columbia River*

The Underwater Wreck

In 1986, a local fisherman discovered the wreck of the *Isabella*. Archaeologists diving into the dangerous, dark waters of the Columbia River found the ship split in half. At times the pow-

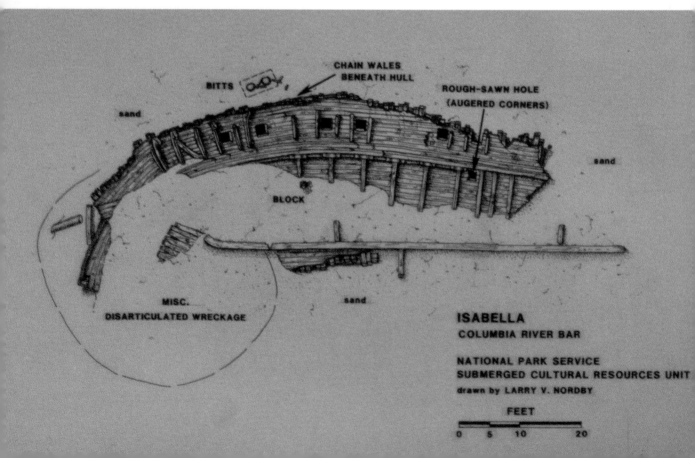

CHAIN WALES
BENEATH HULL

BITTS

ROUGH-SAWN HOLE
(AUGERED CORNERS)

sand

sand

BLOCK

MISC.
DISARTICULATED WRECKAGE

sand

ISABELLA
COLUMBIA RIVER BAR

NATIONAL PARK SERVICE
SUBMERGED CULTURAL RESOURCES UNIT
drawn by LARRY V. NORDBY

FEET

0   5   10   20

erful current pulled the archaeologists off the wreck and swept them downstream. Luckily, the river's freshwater had preserved the ship. **Teredos**, which are undersea worms that eat wood, can't live in freshwater.

The archaeologists found ports—openings on the side of the ship—that the crew had used to save the cargo. The crew was successful, because the archaeologists found only a few scattered pieces of goods. They also found the hole the crew had cut into the ship to pump out the water. Despite 156 years on the bottom, the hole still had splinters all around it where the sailors had hacked at the wood.

The *Isabella* is the oldest wreck that archaeologists on the Pacific Coast have dived on. It reminds us of the days when small ships such as the *Isabella* were the only links for settlers on the frontier to faraway homes in Europe—and how easily those links could be broken.

*The Beaver wrecked
in the late 1880s.*

Chapter Four

The First Steamship in the West

After the wreck of the *Isabella*, Hudson's Bay Company officials decided to build a more powerful ship for their Pacific Coast operations. It would be a steamship with engines and paddle wheels. Because the engines might not always work, this new ship would also have masts and sails.

The *Beaver* was built in London, England, in 1835. It sailed to Fort Vancouver on the Columbia River and arrived in 1836. It was the first steamship to reach the Pacific Coast.

The *Beaver* Arrives

Local Indians carved this picture of the Beaver *in rock.*

The *Beaver* steamed up the coast in hopes of trading for fur. It visited Native American villages never before reached by ship. The steamship impressed the Indians. They even carved a picture of the steamship on the rocks on Vancouver Island near the village of Clo-ose. That rock picture exists to this day.

After fur trading for many years, the *Beaver* carried passengers during the British Columbia Gold Rush of 1858. Then the British Royal Navy used the steamship to survey the coast of British Columbia. Navy officers aboard the *Beaver* named many rocks, islands, and other landmarks on the coast during their voyages. They even named a small group of islands the Innis Islets after the ship's dog.

The *Beaver* was turned into a **tugboat** and finally wrecked near Vancouver, British Columbia, which was just a small logging camp back then. The ship was fifty-three years old. Most ships do not last more than twenty years. When it wrecked, the *Beaver* was already famous as the first steamship on the Pacific Coast, and many people cut pieces off the wreck as souvenirs.

Rock Pictures

Pictures carved into rock are called pictographs. Pictures painted on rocks are called petroglyphs.

Over the years, many people took souvenirs of the first steamship to reach the Pacific Coast.

The *Beaver* Wreck

Archaeologists have been studying the wreck of the *Beaver* for several years. It lies in less than 24 feet (7.3 m) of water near the harbor entrance to Vancouver, now one of the busiest ports in North America. Huge oceangoing ships pass over the *Beaver*'s grave every day. Resting at the bottom is the underside of the steamship's hull with pieces of the engines still inside.

The Beaver *wreck rests in the cold waters of Burrard Inlet near the harbor entrance to Vancouver.*

Archaeologists have learned some interesting things from the *Beaver* wreck. The hull was built strong and heavy to carry the weight of the huge iron engines. Although the *Beaver* had engines, it was built to move through the water like a sailing ship. This was important on a frontier where the engines might break down and might not be repaired for some time.

Archaeologists also found that the *Beaver*'s engines were old-fashioned when they were put into the steamship in 1835.

The Hudson's Bay Company and the shipbuilder apparently felt that an older, simpler engine type was best for the frontier—probably because new parts and major repairs were thousands of miles away. Examining the wreck's engines also revealed a number of repairs and changes over the steamship's long life. Many modifications seem to have been made toward the end of the *Beaver*'s life, when the frontier period was ending and new industries and cities were developing where forests had once stood.

Hard Work

It took the crew of the *Beaver* two days of chopping wood to feed the fires in the engine's boiler to make steam for just one day.

A view of Monterey, which grew into a trading and military center after the Spanish settled California in 1776

Chapter Five

To California by Sea

While the Hudson's Bay Company was busy building forts and sending the *Beaver* up the north Pacific Coast to trade for fur, Mexican settlers in California were trading with visiting ships, most of which were from the United States. Settlers from the United States had begun to cross the plains and the mountains to reach California and Oregon in the late 1830s. By the early 1840s, hundreds were coming every year. Mexican officials feared that these settlers might try to conquer California as their numbers grew larger. Those fears came true in 1846, when the settlers rose up just as the United States and Mexico went to war.

The Gold Rush

Thousands rushed west during the California Gold Rush.

When the war ended in 1848, Mexico lost half of its country, including California, to the United States. California was still a small, "sleepy" land of several thousand people on a distant frontier. But when gold was discovered in the American River

in the heart of California, everything changed. When news of the gold discovery reached the rest of the country—and the world—tens of thousands of people flocked to California. This event was called the California Gold Rush.

Between 1849 and 1850, thousands of people crossed the plains. Many more sailed to California. In all, more than 1,000 ships sailed for San Francisco, the Gold Rush's major port, in 1849. Many people sailed around Cape Horn, at the southern tip of South America, or across the Pacific Ocean. Others sailed to Panama in Central America, hiked across the narrow country, and traveled north by ship.

By 1850, several hundred ships were anchored off San Francisco. Some smaller ships were able to sail up San Francisco Bay to reach the Sacramento and San Joaquin Rivers. If they could sail up the rivers, they could reach the towns of Sacramento and Stockton, the jumping-off points for the gold mines. Thanks to the large number of ships carrying people and goods, California went from frontier land to a heavily populated state with major industries in a matter of a few years.

Wrecks in the Sacramento River

Archaeologists diving in the Sacramento River have discovered the wrecks of four sailing ships that came to California in 1849. These ships had been brought up the river and tied up near the new city of Sacramento. In time, some were deliberately sunk to clear the waterfront, while others were

The Forty-Niners

Because most gold seekers arrived in California in 1849, they were known as the Forty-Niners.

What Type of Ship Is It?

Sailing vessels are divided into types based on the number of masts and the types of sails that they carry:

- A ship is a three-masted vessel with yards that cross each mast carrying a sail. Yards are long tapered wood pieces that support and spread a sail.
- A barque is a three-masted vessel with yards on two of the masts.
- A brig is a two-masted vessel with yards on both masts.
- A schooner is a vessel with masts but no yards. There have been schooners with two, three, four, five, and six masts. There was even one seven-masted schooner.

sunk by the occasional floods that sweep the river.

The most intact or complete wreck is a small two-masted ship, or **brig,** called the *Sterling*. Like many other ships used in the Gold Rush, the *Sterling* was old. Built in Massachusetts in 1833, the tiny brig had sailed to California in 1849 with seven passengers and a cargo of building supplies. While some Gold Rush ships were big and carried many people, most were smaller ships.

The archaeologists found that the *Sterling* had been fixed up to go to California. The hull was covered with new sheets of copper to protect it from teredos. Also found on the wreck was an anchor stamped with the date 1844—eleven years after the *Sterling* was built. Divers were able to wiggle inside the ship to reach the crowded **forecastle,** where the crew had lived. Because the *Sterling* had been stripped after it arrived in Sacramento, only a few broken pieces of pottery remained inside.

Building materials and buildings were scarce and expensive. Like many other ships in California, the *Sterling* had been used as a floating building before it was sunk in 1855. This was no surprise to archaeologists, who were already working on wrecks of other Gold Rush "ship buildings" in San Francisco.

The anchor from the **Sterling**

*The Gold Rush transformed
San Francisco.*

Chapter Six

Floating Buildings

When the Gold Rush started, San Francisco was a small town. Within a year, it was a big, crowded city. Ships arrived daily from around the world. They were filled with passengers and goods. There were not enough places for people to live. Valuable cargoes were stacked up on the docks and in the muddy streets. Because San Francisco was growing so fast, there were not enough buildings. But there were hundreds of ships on the waterfront. Many of them had lost their crews to gold mining. The ships were turned into floating buildings. By 1850, San Francisco was using more than 140 ships as floating warehouses, offices, hotels, and the town jail.

Some ships were pulled right up on the beach. Long wharves and piers were built around them. These ships never went to sea again. As San Francisco continued to grow, the city pushed out from the waterfront. Sand, dirt, and garbage were thrown into the shallow waters of San Francisco Bay to make dry land and many new blocks in downtown San Francisco. This practice also trapped some of the ships that had been pulled ashore or deliberately sunk and covered over.

The Gold Rush ended in 1855. At that time, as many as seventy ships lay buried beneath San Francisco. Since then, construction workers digging in downtown San Francisco have discovered dozens of ships. Archaeologists have studied three of them. The most interesting of these ships was the old whaler *Niantic*.

The *Niantic*

The *Niantic* was hunting whales in the South Pacific Ocean when news of the California gold discovery reached the captain. After sailing to Panama in Central America, the *Niantic* loaded a few hundred passengers and sailed to San Francisco in early 1849. The crew abandoned the ship in San Francisco to hunt for gold.

The captain sold the *Niantic* to three local businessmen who pulled out the ship's masts. They dragged the ship up on

the beach and turned it into a building. The deck was covered over with offices and other rooms. A large door was cut in the side of the ship. The bottom of the *Niantic* was used as a large warehouse.

A large fire in May 1851 burned down most of San Francisco and the *Niantic*. But the bottom of the ship, filled with thousands of artifacts, did not burn. It was buried and a new building was put up on the site. Workers building new structures on the site found the old ship several times. The last discovery was in 1978. People in the city's downtown area often stopped to watch the archaeologists studying the *Niantic*.

After whaling in the South Pacific, the Niantic *was turned into a "ship building," and it was a famous sight in Gold Rush San Francisco.*

City on Fire

San Francisco started out as a town of wood buildings and canvas tents. It burned down several times during the Gold Rush—once at the end of 1849, twice in 1850, twice in 1851, and once in 1852. People started building with brick and iron and formed a volunteer fire department to help prevent the constant fires.

Only the bottom of the ship had survived. It showed that the *Niantic* was a strong, typical ship of the 1830s. Wet mud and sand had preserved thousands of interesting artifacts inside the "ship warehouse." Merchants had used the ship for storage. A crockery merchant had stored plates, bowls, and other dishes. A grocer had stored cans of food, bottles of wine, and champagne from France. A stationery storeowner had stored wooden pencils, books, and bottles of ink. The archae-

ologists also found the bags and trunks that belonged to people who had left the ship to hunt for gold.

The artifacts inside the *Niantic* showed what life had been like in the frontier city. Some of the finds were surprising, such as very expensive wines, food, and other items that came from faraway places such as Paris and London. These artifacts showed archaeologists that San Francisco and California had not been a frontier for long. California's gold attracted many people and they acquired such things as champagne, steam engines, fancy foods, and books that could not have been purchased without the buying power of gold.

Artifacts from the Niantic, *including bottles, nails, an ax, a bayonet, a shovel, and copper sheathing from the hull.*

The busy port of San Francisco welcomed ships from around the world.

Chapter Seven

Trading with the Rest of the World

Throughout the Gold Rush, ships arrived at San Francisco every day. Between 1849 and 1853, 4,753 ships reached San Francisco. Many carried passengers and almost all carried cargo. They carried cargoes from France, England, Australia, China, Hawaii, Mexico, Peru, Panama, and many other countries. Some of the ships were wrecked

Life on a Clipper Ship

Clipper ships had narrow, sharp hulls that cut through water better and carried more sails than other ships. Clipper ships were fast, but they didn't last long. And their crews were worked so hard that many jumped ship when they reached port.

during their voyage. Archaeologists have discovered several of these wrecks. They have studied the remains of two in particular, the *Frolic* and the *Lord Western*.

The *Frolic*

The *Frolic* was a small, fast ship known as a Baltimore **clipper**. This type of clipper and larger clipper ships were popular during the Gold Rush because they could reach California faster than most other ships. The first ship to reach San Francisco with a new cargo was able to sell it at a very high price. Unfortunately for the *Frolic*'s owners, the ship wrecked on its first voyage to California.

When the *Frolic* crashed ashore on the northern California coast in July 1850, no one lived nearby except the local Mitom Pomo Indians. The ship's crew rowed south in a small boat to reach help. The wreck was left to break apart in the sea. The

The Frolic *was a small clipper ship.*

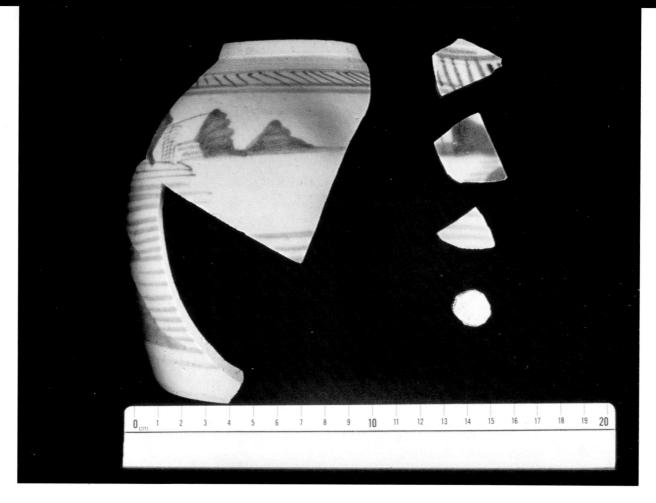

Mitom Pomo **salvaged** many things from the wreck, including blankets and cloth. They used broken bottles to make arrowheads, and they made ornaments and beads from pieces of blue-and-white china bowls and plates. When archaeologists were digging in an old Mitom Pomo village site, they found some of the *Frolic's* cargo. This discovery led them to the wreck.

The *Frolic* had sailed from China with ginger packed in jars, camphor trunks, beer, Chinese furniture, jewelry, guns —and a house. The house was prefabricated. That means it was built, taken apart, numbered, and packed. Workers in

At left is a large section of a ginger jar excavated from the Frolic site. At right are the shards that the Mitom Pomo made into beads.

45

A musket, three pistols, and four pieces of a sword were found at the Frolic *wreck.*

California would unpack the house and put it back together, piece by piece. Many prefabricated houses were shipped to California from China during the Gold Rush. Only one of these Chinese prefabricated houses survives today, so archaeologists were excited to discover evidence of a prefabricated house in the *Frolic* wreck.

By studying the wreck and the cargo, archaeologists are learning more about Gold Rush trade between China and California. The bottom of the *Frolic*, filled with rusted iron bars and three anchors, lies in a small cove in shallow water. Much of the cargo was porcelain bowls. Broken pottery lies everywhere on the bottom. Artifacts collected from the wreck include bottles, guns, pottery, oyster-shell windows from the prefabricated house, parts of camphor trunks, and pieces of the ship.

The *Lord Western*

Farther up the Pacific Coast in Canada, archaeologists have discovered another Gold Rush wreck. The *Lord Western* was an English ship that first sailed to California in 1852 with nearly 300 Chinese immigrants. In 1853, the ship was sent north to British Columbia.

There in the middle of the thick forest, loggers were cutting down trees and selling them to California merchants. Lumber for building houses, docks, and piers was in demand. The *Lord Western* loaded a cargo of logs in early December 1853 and headed south for San Francisco. A storm pushed the half-flooded ship ashore on Vancouver Island, where divers discovered the wreck in 1957.

Archaeologists excavated the wreck in 1987. They found many of the logs still inside the ship. They also found the captain's telescope and a Chinese bowl left behind by an immigrant. The wreck of the *Lord Western*, like the *Frolic*, reminded archaeologists that many countries traded with California. The California Gold Rush opened up the western frontier to the world.

The captain's telescope from the Lord Western

47

After the Gold Rush, steamboats such as the Arabia filled the riverways.

Chapter Eight

The End of the Frontier

When the California Gold Rush ended in 1855, both North American coasts were settled and had large cities, farms, and factories. Although the westward movement continued, many people stopped and settled down in the plains and prairies instead of pushing on to the Pacific Coast. Railroads brought many people west. Others traveled by river into the heart of North America on riverboats powered with steam engines.

Some of the riverboats—including the *Arabia* and the *Bertrand*—wrecked and sank into the muddy waters. The rivers sealed these boats and their cargoes in thick mud, which served as an excellent preservative. Archaeologists working on the wrecks discovered boxes and crates that had writing on them and were still nailed shut. They found bags and trunks filled with clothes still folded and packed. And they found food—stored in bottles, jars, and barrels—that could still be eaten, if anyone wanted to try.

The *Arabia*

The steamer *Arabia* sank in the Missouri River near Kansas City, Missouri, in 1856 after hitting a **snag**. The river moved in later years, leaving the wreck buried under a cornfield in the old riverbed. It was discovered and excavated between 1988 and 1989.

Thousands of artifacts were found, still packed in barrels and crates. Today, the *Arabia* Steamboat Museum in Kansas City displays the clothing, tools, farming equipment, food, hardware, and other artifacts from the wreck. Museum visitors can see everything settlers brought with them to the frontier.

Visitors to the Arabia Steamboat Museum can view clothes, shoes, hats, and blankets from the underwater site.

The *Bertrand*

The wreck of the steamer *Bertrand* was also found under a farmer's field in an old riverbed. The *Bertrand* ripped its hull and sank in the Missouri River, just north of Omaha, Nebraska, in 1865. The American Civil War was ending, and

Archaeologists discovered the remains of the Bertrand *under 30 feet (9 m) of clay and sand.*

settlers were once again moving west. The 162-foot (49-m)-long *Bertrand* was carrying settlers, their baggage, and cargo to the Montana frontier. It hit a tangle of logs in the water and sank. Everyone got off safely, and parts of the riverboat—the top and the engines—were salvaged. But the rest of the wreck quickly sank into the mud and disappeared.

The *Bertrand* wreck was discovered in 1967. Archaeologists completely excavated the old boat and removed tens of thousands of artifacts. They were amazed to find that boxes and crates still had writing on them. Jars and bottles had paper labels stuck to them. Inside the baggage of one frontier family were clothes and a small slate that the daughter had used in her school lessons. Because paper was expensive, children did all of their lessons on small blackboards called slates.

Riverboats built after the *Arabia* and the *Bertrand* brought more settlers. Railroads brought even more people. Cities grew up where small frontier towns once stood. By the end of the 1800s, San Francisco, Portland, Chicago, Seattle, Kansas City, and Omaha in the United States as well as Van-

This bottle of pickled vegetables from the Bertrand *was submerged for more than 100 years.*

Learning about Riverboats

Thousands of riverboats were built for the frontier. Most lasted only a few years. The wreck of the *Arabia* and the *Bertrand* (above) told archaeologists that these riverboats were big, flat rafts with simple steam engines. Large paddle wheels at the back pushed the boats. They were big enough to carry many people and tons of cargo. Snags, such as those that sank the *Arabia* and the *Bertrand*, were everywhere on the Missouri River. The owners did not seem to care about saving the cargoes. They did work hard to save the most valuable part of the boat— the steam engine.

couver and Winnipeg in Canada were all growing urban centers. The western frontier had grown up. But lying in the rivers, lakes, and ocean were the wrecks of the ships that had extended the frontier west.

Glossary

archaeologists—scientists who study past cultures based on artifacts and other evidence left behind

artifacts—things made by humans

brig—a square-rigged sailing ship with two masts

clipper—a fast-sailing ship with tall masts and large sails

excavate—to scientifically recover and study the remains of past human activity

expedition—a journey for a specific purpose

forecastle—the crew's quarters in a ship's bow

hull—the frame or body of a ship

rapids—parts of a river where the current flows fast, usually over rocks

rudder—a flat movable section located at the back of a ship and used for steering

salvage—to recover or save, especially from wreckage

snag—a tree branch stuck underwater and not visible from the surface

teredos—undersea worms that eat wood

tugboat—a powerful boat used to tow and push other boats

To Find Out More

Books

Bentley, Judith. *Explorers, Trappers, and Guides*. Brookfield, Conn.: Twenty-First Century, 1995.

Blumberg, Rhoda. *The Incredible Journey of Lewis and Clark*. New York: Peter Smith, 1999.

Collins, James. *Settling the American West*. New York: Franklin Watts, 1993.

Ketchum, Liza. *The Gold Rush*. Boston: Little, Brown, 1996.

Landau, Elaine. *The Pomo*. New York: Franklin Watts, 1994.

Nirgiotis, Nicholas. *West by Waterway: Rivers and U.S. Expansion*. Danbury, Conn.: Franklin Watts, 1995.

Stein, R. Conrad. *The California Gold Rush*. Danbury, Conn.: Children's Press, 1995.

Organizations and Online Sites

The *Arabia* Steamboat Museum
400 Grand Boulevard
Kansas City, MO 64108
http://www.1856.com
This museum and website display artifacts from the *Arabia* wreck.

Canadian Museum of Civilization
100 Laurier Street
P.O. Box 3100
Station B, Hull, Quebec J8X 4H2, Canada
http://www.civilization.ca/membrs/canhist/canoe/can00eng.html
This museum has done extensive work on native craft, particularly canoes.

DeSoto National Wildlife Refuge
U.S. Fish and Wildlife Service
1434 316th Lane
Missouri Valley, IA 51555
http://refuges.fws.gov/NWRSFiles/CulturalResources/Bertrand/Bertrand.html
This visitor center and website display the *Bertrand* artifacts.

Museum of the City of San Francisco
2801 Leavenworth Street
San Francisco, CA 94133
http://www.sfmuseum.org/hist1/index2.html
This museum and website provide information about San Francisco and the California Gold Rush.

San Francisco Maritime National Historical Park
Fort Mason Center
San Francisco, CA 94123
http://www.nationalparks.org/guide/parks/san-francisc-1699.htm
This museum and website tell the story of the *Niantic* and other Gold Rush ships and display the *Niantic* artifacts.

Vancouver Maritime Museum
1905 Ogden Avenue
Vancouver, BC, V6J 1A3, Canada
http://www.vmm.bc.ca
This museum and website have many pieces of the *Beaver*, including the boiler, on display.

A Note on Sources

Like most authors, I have my own way of researching when I write a book. I usually start in the library. Public libraries are great places because even if they do not have the book you are looking for, they can search other libraries online and find it for you.

I also check scientific journals and popular magazines for related articles. *Archaeology* magazine, published by the Archaeological Institute of America, was particularly useful. This publication is online at *www.archaeology.org*.

I also talked to other archaeologists who work around the world on shipwrecks and other sites. They offered hints, gave suggestions of people to speak with, and directed me to Internet sites. Most of the archaeologists I know are always willing to answer questions and help other researchers and students. That is how I learned more about the steamboat *Arabia*.

—*James P. Delgado*

Index

Numbers in *italics* indicate illustrations.

About the Author

James P. Delgado has worked as a park ranger, a historian, an underwater archaeologist, a teacher, and a museum director. His love of archaeology began when he was ten, and he went on his first dig at age fourteen. Today, he is the executive director of Vancouver Maritime Museum.

James P. Delgado has written eighteen books related to history and underwater archaeology. He is also the author of the Watts Library books *Native American Shipwrecks* and *Wrecks of American Warships*. He currently lives in Vancouver, British Columbia.